Living An Abundant Life Within Your Means

By James Nugent

Please note that all prices are estimates. As the cost of everything continues to skyrocket the principles behind the examples will remain the same.

So, many of us are on our last financial legs. Most of us spent our adult lives assuring ourselves that as long as we work for a living we will prosper. Some of us smugly thought that people in poverty probably deserved it because they are lazy.

Then the economy turned on the middle and upper middle class. Then suddenly, it wasn't possible to always find a job that provided a suitable amount of money to maintain our chosen lifestyle. After that millions of our generation became the new poor.

A strange thing happened after coming to accept the new economy. The new poor had little or no poverty survival skills. Things that might be obvious to a child of poverty eluded the new poor.

This book comes from a shocking discovery I made while watching a TV cooking show about decade or so ago. The show was about how to make cheap and savory meals for the whole family for under $8 a person. At the time I was just finishing off a delightful and filling meal that cost less that a dollar (see details in food chapter). I calculated my food expenses for the day. Yup I spent under $2 dollars for the day. Wow it hit me. If people think that $8 a meal per person is living inexpensively; then they are being set up for absolute disaster and disappointment if they are forced into minimum wage or part time work.

It also occurred to me that even if one doesn't lose their job and their house; they might just spend their lives as wage slave to credit cards, loans and mortgage. I quickly did the math and discovered that I would personally spend the next 34 years paying off my debts if I didn't change my spending habits and attitude. That's when I started to think outside the box. It was a box or cage made from attachment to wasteful behaviors habits and attitude.

If you have a sneaky suspicion that you can live a healthy, productive and inexpensive lifestyle; read on and entertain some of the following ideas.

An Analogy.

How Big is The Hole in Your Boat?

I live on the beach in southern Puget Sound. When I put a new boat at anchor in our lagoon, I noticed about a cup of seawater had leaked in through the hull. A friend said, "don't worry about it. It's such a small whole in the boat." I forgot to check the boat in the morning, and that evening as I drove to my home I could see that boat had completely flooded and sunk. Fortunately the lagoon goes dry at most low tides!

This state of affairs is similar to wasteful spending. Even a tiny amount of waste over time will be a huge financial loss.

For example, if I buy lunch out and a couple cups of coffee through the day I could easily spend $10 a day. No big deal right? No and yes. So $70 per week multiplied by 52 weeks a year costs you equals $3640 a year. Still thinking No big deal? I will show you 10-20 ways you can save money in a single day. The savings can add up to around $20+ or a lot more a day. Twenty dollars a day multiplied by 365 days gives you $7,280 a year or $72,800 in ten years plus any interest you make on savings account interest.

That is money you would have wasted. That is money you can't get paid interest for by putting it in the bank. All of a sudden small wasteful habits mean you don't have money to survive if your company is downsized or goes out of business. Extended out 40 years, $20 dollars a day results in more than a ¼ million dollars for retirement. So even tiny amounts of waste like a tiny hole in a boat can lead to or allow a disaster.

By living frugally during tough times and easy times we can develop a lifestyle that makes financial sense and is a pleasure to engage fully.

The rest of this book will address potential strategies for reducing your overhead without taking the joy out of life. It may require adjustments in your lifestyle but what choice do you have? People who wouldn't face adjustments in their lifestyle have actually killed themselves. If it gets too stressful for you, get competent mental and spiritual help.

The Scenario

Let's say for the purposes of discussion that your household income is cut in half. It matters not what the cause. Be it a divorce, death of a spouse, employer bankruptcy or being fired; the net result is that you now have ½ the income with which you are accustomed. It is past time to start thinking outside the box. So face up to the facts. You may have to move to a lower cost shelter even if you have kids. If you can't pay the monthly taxes, rent or mortgage, sooner or later somebody will forcibly evict you from your home. This is survival mode time.

How ever you solve the housing issue you still need to get food, clothing, transportation to work or interviews, and reliable means for communicating with employers and potential employers.

We will discuss the shelter issue in the shelter chapter but unless you rationally address the other issues which cause you to hemorrhage money nothing will really change for you. Your crisis may even escalate into homelessness.

I have relied on my wife's expertise for the discussion about food. She has mastered the art of inexpensive shopping and cooking. She was also heavily involved in the discussion about technology and entertainment media.

Hang on for a wild discussion on what to do when you are short on money!

Chapter One

Food and How to Get it Inexpensively

If times are tough, call 211 and get the times and days for when the local food banks are open. Don't feel bad about getting free food just be sure to remember to donate food and money when you have some in the future.

Please don't use food banks unless you really need them. If you drink or smoke or gamble; I really don't think it is fair that you also consume the food that children need for growth and brain development.

Discount grocery stores are great resources for those in poverty or wanting to live frugally. Why buy the exact same product that may cost 5 times as much across the street at regular grocery stores when it can be had inexpensively at the discount store? Just be sure read the expiration date of the product. I have never found an expired product on the shelf at a discount store but I have seen a few products with no expiration date and these I have avoided.

Coupons, and electronic coupons and sales are serious saving opportunities. Generic and house brands can often also save much money on the food budget. Depending what we buy, we often save 50%-75% on our food budget. We make a game out of create healthy meals for very little money.

My wife and I have completely different food preferences and dietary needs and restrictions. For example I am a pescatarian (a fish eating vegetarian) and have an assortment medical restriction on what I can eat. Still she reads the labels and finds health promoting vegetarian foods that I like.

For 20 years I was a "junk food" vegetarian. I ate everything except land dwelling animals. I ate very poorly and it is expensive to buy pizza and peal the meat off of it
:>

Besides being revolted by animal meat and its' by products; I became a vegetarian of sorts because it just seemed wrong to use 21 pounds a grain in order to make one pound of cow meat. It seemed more just to abstain in the hopes that the grain would be used to feed the poor. We do produce enough grain to feed the rest of the planet, if we would not waste it on cows.

Be that as it may; you don't need to be a vegetarian in order to live frugally. My wife is a: steak, hamburger, sausage, and bacon kind of eater and we live well at very little expense.

The freezer

Having enough freezer space is a major key to living inexpensively. I bought one for $50 at a garage sale. We keep it filled with bread we get form the bread store. The bread store is a wonderful place where we get bread that will be old in a few days. I have a second freezer we fill with all sorts of typical frozen foods that we get from the discount stores and any wild foods I harvest from the garden, the woods, the yard and or Puget Sound. My wife keeps her meats in the refrigerator freezer. I rarely have to look at it.

Wild foods.

I dehydrate, eat or freeze everything I harvest. In the fall I can get my fish right at the commercial fishing dock. Cheap Salmon can be as low as a dollar or two per fish. I usually give a tip to have them cleaned. Crab are free for the price of a license and a crab pot out on the bay. Getting to my crab pot is done in an inflatable toy raft. Delightful large colorful mushrooms grow in my yard in such abundance that I dehydrate them and have quart jars of these tasty tidbits all year. Blackberries grow like weeds behind my house and provide us with privacy and a natural fence that nobody is willing to climb over! I pick and freeze up 10 pies worth of berries every Summer. Every year I try to grow a garden.

It is amazing what you can grow in a 10' by 10' plot of land. I have been very successful with squash and onions and mint. We have very sandy soil. So since I am a lazy gardener other foods are usually produced sparingly. The mint is for fresh tea. It is so good I often brew a jug of tea and a save it in the refrigerator for days. I am trying to grow my own fruit trees but my friendly neighbors are happy to share their surplus. Dehydrators are crucial for having free year round fruit and fruit leather. My favorite fruit products are banana chips and apple bits. Often I can get an entire grocery box of ripe fruit from a local store for a couple bucks and then dehydrate everything. It will keep for a year if store in a cool dark dry place.

Wherever you live there are opportunities to harvest something. My grandmother who lived in Seattle WA taught me about harvesting in the city. Using container gardening and vacant lots and her own '10 by 10' plot of land she enjoyed the seasons too.

This left in me a permanent awareness of the natural environment and its' produce even in the city. One of my favorite dishes which grandma would make was wilted dandelion salad. These days I steam some dandelion leaves, and clover flowers from the yard and throw a little olive oil on it.

There is something nice about living a little off the land and of course it is free!

An Example of An Inexpensive Breakfast.

The easiest meal of the day is breakfast. Just spend $2 at the dollar or other discount grocery type store. For $2 dollars you can get 30 servings of oatmeal and 30 servings cream of wheat. That makes the centerpiece of breakfast about 9 cents a serving.
I gather various berries through the Summer, and Fall. I freeze them for use on my cereal. The small chest freezer cost $50 at garage sale. Bread for breakfast toast comes from the discount bread store. Bread from the discount bread store costs $1 dollar a loaf and can be frozen until we need it. Real cheap bread is made for toast at breakfast and lunch sandwiches in my bread making machine and cost around 60 cents a loaf. The machine cost me $5 at a thrift store 10 years ago. They can still found at garage sales. Fruit for breakfast and lunch often comes from my neighbor's trees for free and I dehydrate them in several machines I got for $6 a piece at a thrift store. If I want yogurt or kefir I just make it in my dehydrator at 10 cents a serving instead of $2 a serving. I buy some yogurt at the grocery discount store then produce at least 30- 40 servings from just one serving. Another treat is yogurt cheese spread made by hanging a quart of yogurt in a cheese cloth over a bowl over night. Throw in some herbs picked from my garden and it makes a wonderful spread for bread or dip. A favorite breakfast food that Theresa will stock up on when

it is on sale, is "substitute egg product" (egg whites). She will make totally healthy egg white omelets. She will buy 10 or 15 boxes at 25 cents to $1.50 at a grocery discount store, and then we freeze them until we want them. This supply lasts for months.

The whole idea is to eat something healthy and cheap for breakfast. Just forget about the typical greasy gut bomb breakfast that cost $6 a plate. Don't ever indulge in process breakfast cereal. They are ridiculously expensive 4 or 5 dollars a box. They are also often laden with sugar and don't provide the nutrition you want. Breakfast rarely costs me more than 60 cents.

The idea is to take advantage of sales and alternative stores which sell healthy staple items.

Lunch-
Lunch is a huge budget killer if you don't make your own. I usually have leftovers from the night before and or a sandwich, and some fruit. The fruit can be dehydrated or fresh. Never buy bottled water. It is often just tap water anyway but some of the plastic bottles turn out to be a health risk. Use a safe water jug or canteen. Bottled water is a ridiculous expense. I do have a friend who distills his own water from city tap water for pennies a gallon because he doesn't trust city water, which can contain fluoride and chlorine.

Dinner –

Eating is more than an act of taking in nutrition. It can be a social time and a bonding time. When weather permits we enjoy a BBQ. Usually we just cook inside the house. If we are cooking a salmon (bought for a few dollars) my wife leaves the oven door open after it is turned off to provide a bit of supplemental heat in the house.

Whatever we cook for dinner, we make enough to supply several meals. Salmon "leftovers" become lunch sandwiches for the next day and some of it may be frozen for future use. This saves cooking time and electricity.

If it is summer or fall perhaps I cook a couple squash from the garden in the same oven while we are baking the fish. The leftover squash also become lunch the next day. Once in a while I stuff bits of scraps of squash and fish into a large Bolletes mushroom from the yard and bake it well. It is a special treat. The whole idea is to make it fun and cheap.

Speaking of inexpensive, we often get spaghetti or even rice in bulk and cook up 8 or 10 servings for a dollar or two. The other day I saw 25lb bags of rice for $8. My wife makes sure the pasta doesn't contain semolina, which is highly processed and she feels it might be unhealthy for me. Leftovers are always saved for the next day or frozen for future use.

I do two more things to cut costs. I sprout all kinds of beans to make a cheap bean sprout salad for lunch and dinner. I also sometimes make my own vegetable burger patties by cooking chic peas, or red or black beans; mashing them, seasoning them to taste, adding flour, and frying them in olive oil. These are supper cheap and healthy. They make fine lunch sandwiches or dinner BBQ burgers.

Weight Loss Diets

I only know of one diet that really works. Go to the American Diabetic Association website and take a close look at their weight loss diet. Diabetes is a degenerative and progressive ultimately fatal disease. It is hormonally based and the victims can die early. The key to longevity is diet, exercise and stress management. As a group diabetics know and live weight management. What they promote works and can be done on a tiny budget. Other diets are generally expensive and sometimes unhealthy.

Chapter 2

Shelter is a Place to Call Home.

Here is the deal. If you are being foreclosed because you can't afford to pay the mortgage, seriously consider packing up and then wait until the bank demands you leave. This will keep you sheltered until the inevitable. Any income you might still have can be saved up to pay for a rental. Also the banks have been so slow to foreclose recently that it may take a couple years to take away your home. That's free housing until you must leave. I have a friend who spent 18 months living in his former home with his 3 children for free. At $1900 a month he was able to get a nest egg, which supported his new frugal lifestyle.

If you rent, seriously consider leaving as soon as you know you are about to default on the agreement. After all the landlord can't rent it out while you are still living there and it will just run up how much you owe her if she sues you for breaking the contract.

So if you find yourself without shelter, hopefully you do have a tiny bit of money. If you can't move in with relatives start thinking outside the box. Who do you know who has an RV or a boat in the marina? Perhaps you can rent it for cheap. Perhaps you can buy a derelict boat for a few hundred dollars and live in the marina.

Once after graduate school, I bought a boat for $50 a month (for 12 months) and lived on it for years. I took the money I saved on housing and traveled to exotic places around the world many times. I later sold the boat for $300 to a live aboard family who wanted a separate bedroom for their teenage daughter. Families often live in marinas but most often it is a divorced male who got the boat in the settlement.

I am presently working on a book about how I lived aboard for 12 years. It is cheap, easy, exotic and fun.

If you can buy or borrow an RV find somebody with private property. Live there for a modest fee or free. The RV doesn't even have to run just have it towed there. Better yet live at the lake at an RV Park. It costs a little more but you will have electricity and water. Perhaps a friend will let you plug an extension cord into her house. If the RV runs just dump the toilet holding tank properly elsewhere.

I had a friend who lived at the airport in a defunct flying boat. They liked him being there so much that they paid him to keep an eye all the other planes. This arrangement lasted for years and gave him something to put on his resume. He then worked at the mall for another twenty years as a security guard.

There are thousands of summer camps that need seasonal and or year round live in maintenance people. Families are often welcome in these positions. Marinas need live in managers. Apartments need live in managers. Trailer parks need live in managers. I even have a friend who house sits for people year round. She goes from one beautiful home to another all year. She gets to see new scenery and gets paid to do it. There are also clean and safe trailer homes for really little money if you ask around. My point is think outside the house (box) when you are hit by hard times.

Please note if you don't change you behavior and habits of spending; you will still have money problems even if you find a place to live for free.

Chapter 3

Clothing is Proper Costuming

Poverty does not have to look trashy.
People do judge a book by its' cover. Since this is true always bathe and groom yourself when you appear in public. You never know when you might run into a potential employer. As the weeks and months pass by you might feel it is ok to get a little sloppy but remember that the world of work, which you want to re-enter hasn't even noticed that you are gone! Whatever you do you; you do not want to look like a homeless person. Attend free community events, church events and do volunteer work.

If you look and act employable sooner or later some options will show themselves.

Always carry business cards and a resume' with you or in the car even if you are going to the local grocery store. Dress the part you really want to play. Always be courteous and kind. Be the kind of person that people want around.

Business clothing can be found in clothing banks and thrift stores. I bought my favorite "going to an interview suit" on my way to an interview for a counseling job. It cost me $15 at a thrift store and an identical model costs $500 today. I also borrowed a pair of $200 Italian black loafers from a friend. I got the job on the spot. That job lasted 8 years before I took a high school Spanish Teacher job. Again I dressed the part and was hired on the spot and I didn't even have an appointment for interview.

After leaving that job I dressed the part and interviewed for a job that wasn't even advertised. I was again hired on the spot and spent the most rewarding professional year of my life as an alternative high school counselor! People do really judge a book by its' cover.

Plot and plan how you should dress. Gather the props and practice wearing and using the props until it feels normal and natural to you. Enjoy being yourself while reinventing yourself. Of course the same principles go for women. Be sure to dress the part with extra thought given to looking conservative.

When I lived on a boat in the marina for 12 years I had two airtight plastic tubs. My clothing was always fresh and did not have that living on a boat scent.

Chapter 4

Communications and living in a digital world.

Few things are more personal than what we do for entertainment, information, and communication. If you can find a new paradigm; a less expensive way of meeting your wants and needs, you will know how to cut overhead extensively.

I grew up at the beginning of cell phones, cable TV, and personal computers. This has shaped my fascination with modern technology.

At one time I had a cell phone the size of a shoes box. It came from Radio Shack, cost $300 and resided in my $300 dollar used Buick. It cost $1 a minute to make calls in 1989. It felt normal for me to have a way to call people when I chose to do so.

I grew up in a family that was in the top 1% of income earners in the late 1970's. In our home that sold for more than a million dollars 10 years ago; I was accustomed to watching Showtime TV and all of the other possible movie services. Even when I later lived aboard small 22' boats in marinas around Puget Sound I got cable as soon as it was available. I just didn't feel like it was home until I had cable TV. Now I have a new attitude. That new attitude has made all the difference financially.

Yes, we probably need communication and information tools in order to be involved and responsible citizens but entertainment is truly optional. We can easily develop optional entertainment methods and sometimes we can still use digital technology to be amused for free.

Cell phones

If you have cell phones get rid of the landline. Cell phones are vastly more expensive but sometimes there is no practical way to get rid of the cell phones for a year or two because you are trapped into a contract. Then again I suggest that you ditch the contract phones as soon as possible and use pay as you go phones. There are now "pay as you go programs" which now provide the same features that cell phone contracts now provide, for about half the cost! If you reduce the features you can even save more.

Children and Cell Phones

No child should have internet access on their phone. It can cost $30 to $60+ a month ($360 to $720+ a year) just for the data package! I have a friend who has 3 teenage children. She was paying $2160+
a year for children's cell phones. When one of this single parents' children "needed" an upgrade, mom asked me what to do. I went over to their beautiful home and asked the kids, "what is the purpose of a cell phone?" After much debate and some manipulation on my part it was decided that there were two purposes for a cell phone. The cell phone was for calling mom for safety reasons and to chat unsupervised with friends.

Mom decided that she didn't want to pay for unsupervised cell talk/texting. The children were shocked. One orangutan even threatened to call the police or CPS! Mom eventually decided to pay for only two pay as you go phones. Most pay as you go phones cost $10 a month for certain services. If the child would like more services they can pay for them.

In this story both children decided to pay an extra $10 a month out of their "own" money in order to have a text service. The other child would have to live without a phone. He never did call the police or CPS, but he did go against his wishes, to an out of state treatment program.

Don't be bullied into to paying your children's cell phone bills.

Newspapers

Go get your local information on line for free or cheap. We read our local paper online daily with the Safari browser. Other browsers seem to be overrun with popup ads.

TV News

We can watch our local news online for free. It is just one channel but we have found that all the local news channels seem to be the same. A plus in using online local news is that we can view newscasts any time we want. We never miss the news!

Movies and TV Shows

Oh my goodness there are so many options for movie watching. We have chosen Netflix at this time. We pay Less than $10 a month and we get all the movies we want online. TV shows are now available, often for free online.

Books For Reading.

Public libraries are great for free reading of magazines and books.

I have also participated in cooperative where I bought used books and then after reading them, gave them back to the stores for credit on more books. This was an agreeable arrangement but since I usually read at least 2 books a week it was getting expensive. So I switched to E-books on Kindle. The first thing that attracted me to the Kindle reader, was that one could put "free books" into the search engine and have access to one million free books.
The reader cost me $69 dollars and paid for itself in five months.

Chapter 5

Credit cards and what to do?

We got rid of all are credit card debt before we got married. When we got credit card offers we had my stepsons chop up the cards. At one point we were offered $100,000 in credit. My wife and I are convinced that credit dept is a form of modern day indentured servitude or slavery. With even small cards it can take decades to pay them off.

A friend once asked us, "but what about emergencies?" I said we live within are means and will just pay in cash. Cash seems to work everywhere. If we want to buy something on the internet we use prepaid debit cards. Debit cards work well for hotels and plane tickets too.

The whole credit card system seems to be rigged against the consumer and we choose not to participate.
The last car I bought, I paid $7,000 in cash and since it gets regular maintenance it is coming up on ¼ million miles. When it finally dies, I will just buy another one with cash.

What about a mortgage? We live in a modest modular home on the beach on southern Puget Sound. We really enjoy our home, which we bought on a five year owner contract.

We put view windows in it and will eventually complete some well planned energy efficiency upgrades. I'm not saying everybody should live in a modular home but I am saying that living simply has really made financial sense for us and now that it is paid off we will have extra money for savings, retirements, cars, and vacations.

Chapter 6

Transportation- alternative, public, and private

When you decided to live where you live, one consideration must have been how you would get to work. I recently tried to rent my office near my home but in the end my electric assist bicycle would not do the job.

Still every time I can ride the bike or take the bus I can save money.

Please think outside the box. Can you walk, run or cycle to work? Can you row or telecommute to work? Cut your transportation expenses.

A Four Day Work Week

You can cut 20% off your weekly transportation bill by only working 4 days @10 hours a day? Find out if it is possible at your work.

Working From Home

What if you can save 40% a week on transportation expenses by working at home two days a week from your computer? Please think and talk about it. If all your costs for transportation and parking were $400 month; it would save you $160 a month and $768,000 over a 40 year professional lifetime.

Get creative with transportation and maybe start a carpool!

Chapter 7

Recreation.

I have learned from watching my friends and associates, that a period of unemployment is typically a bad time for everyone involved. So much of our personal self esteem seems to be based upon what we own and how much money we make.

Besides using 8 hours a day searching for work; unemployed people need to spend much time each day doing meaningful/productive and fun activity.

Forget about online gaming or chatting with cam girls. I can almost guarantee that this sort of activity will destroy your budget and your marriage. What I mean is do something that will improve your physical health, spiritual health, mental health, social health or financial situation every day! Nope you still must get up bathe and produce something everyday.

In 2003 I spent 6 months unemployed. It was an extraordinary challenge for me but I made the rule about doing meaningful daily activity, and it turned out well. When it was over I was improved in many areas and even more employable! In a strange way the burden of unemployment morphed into time off for self improvement.

Things to do When Unemployed

-Spend at least 8 hours a day networking and searching for work. Be willing to except anything.

-Volunteer at the church, the YMCA, or anywhere you can use or develop skills.

-Take free online classes. Learn more about your chosen profession or gain new skills.

-Walk, run, bicycle or swim.

-Read a book, learn a new language, make your off work time profitable

-Do something creative: learn to draw portraits, or write a book about being unemployed and upload it to Amazon.com for free, learn to play the guitar and sing for tips at open mike night at the local bar. Try starting your own business.

Chapter 7

Things not to do when unemployed.

-You can't afford to smoke, drink, or gamble. You cannot waste precious resources on addictive behaviors. If giving up these behaviors is a problem for you get free help by calling 211.

-You cannot afford drive fast you can't afford traffic tickets and wasting gas. Besides, you could have an accident and end up in the hospital, or get sued by somebody.

-If you don't have a pet dog or cat you can't afford one now. Having a pet may also limit your housing opportunities and you will need to buy pet food and vet services.

Chapter 8

Radical Self Imposed frugality

Using the financial resources you have, in a wise and frugal manner does not mean being deprived. Instead a simplified life can be much healthier and happier. A lifestyle of chasing after the all mighty dollar and all the material things money can buy; will always in the long run be a sad ending. When you live within your means and put people first in your life, the reward is peace of heart.

When you are not distracted, by hoarding money, and material goods; you begin to think about the needs of others. Then you will begin to discover ways to help others. Practicing the art of helping others becomes a most rewarding lifestyle. Always give to the poor even when you are poor. You will be blessed.

Chapter 9

Peace of Mind Through Finding God

If you live be human rules you will feel much anxiety in times of economic trouble. If you align your behaviors and attitudes with God; you will not only be able to manage the stressors but also find comfort and solace. Ask God what to do in even the most intimate issues and he will guide and support you.

He will forgive you when you sin and heal you of what you have done to yourself. Our God is a most generous God who knows what we need and what we want. When our wants are good for us and will move us closer to salvation he will grant our desires. When our wants are not good for us he will not enable our dysfunctional behavior and attitudes although we are free to continue our misery. Pray contently for wisdom joy and peace.

A Prayer

May God bless us always and in His time someday bring us
to eternal life.

May the Lord comfort us in times of need and want, and
teach us always to thankful.

Final Questions and Answers

Q. Do you really harvest food from your yard, woods
and garden?

A. Yes and it really does taste delicious!

Q. How can you really get Salmon for a dollar or two?

A. Go to the marinas where the fish buyers meet.

Q. But I would never feel right being frugal.

A. Simplicity is an acquired lifestyle. Pray for it.

Q. How do I think outside the box?

A. Start by letting your imagination run wild!

Q. Is it fun to be frugal and live more simply?

A. To be free of slavery to money is great!

Q. What are you writing about next?

A. Check Amazon.com and find out.

Other books by James Nugent

-An Alternative Boating Guide to Southern Puget Sound

-How I sailed from Olympia to The San Juan Islands and Returned Safely

-The Rainbow Road And Other Signs Of God's Love

Available in paperback, Kindle E-book, and Audible Book formats at Amazon.com

www.ingramcontent.com/pod-product-compliance
Lightning Source LLC
Chambersburg PA
CBHW071600170526
45166CB00004B/1741